A WHORE'S MANIFESTO

Also by Kay Kassirer

Confessions of a Queer

Unbandage the Wounds

A WHORE'S MANIFESTO

An Anthology of Writing and Artwork by Sex Workers

Edited by Kay Kassirer

with a foreword by Clementine von Radics

Thorntree  Press

A Whore's Manifesto
An Anthology of Writing and Artwork by Sex Workers

Thorntree Press, LLC
P.O. Box 301231
Portland, OR 97294
press@thorntreepress.com

Thorntree Press's editorial offices are located on the ancestral, traditional and unceded lands of the Musqueam, Squamish and Tsleil-Waututh nations.

Cover design by Siana Sonoquie
Interior design by Jeff Werner
Copy-editing by Heather van der Hoop
Proofreading by Hazel Boydell

Library of Congress Cataloging-in-Publication Data
  Names: Kassirer, Kay, editor.
  Title: A whore's manifesto : an anthology of writing and artwork by sex workers / edited by Kay Kassirer ; with a foreword by Clementine von Radics.

  Description: Portland, OR : Thorntree Press, [2019]
  Identifiers: LCCN 2019013314| ISBN 9781944934897 (pbk.) | ISBN 9781944934910
  (kindle) | ISBN 9781944934927 (pdf)
  Subjects: LCSH: Prostitutes. | Prostitution. | Sex.
  Classification: LCC HQ118 .W46 2019 | DDC 306.74dc23
  LC record available at https://lccn.loc.gov/2019013314

10 9 8 7 6 5 4 3

Printed in the United States of America.

Contents

Acknowledgments

Thank you to my blood family.
To my mother, who always supported my writing, and now
watches over me and guides me through this world.
To my father, who tries his best to understand, and loves
me endlessly.
To my sister, a continual reminder of the good that exists within
both humanity and myself.

Thank you to my poetry family.
To Charlie Petch, for pushing me to start writing about sex work.
To Rabbit Richards, soul sibling, teammate, and best friend.
To Łapḥsṗaṫunakʔi Łiṁaqsti, also known as Mitcholos Touchie,
a powerful presence who teaches me so much.
To Vanessa McGowan, for empowering me to share my story.
To Jess Tollestrup, for helping me edit, and loving me for who
I am.

Thank you to Thorntree Press for believing in this book and in
our stories.

Thank you to all of the sex workers I have shared space with,
learned from, pretended to fuck, and genuinely loved.

Foreword

Sex work can be many things. Phone sex, camming, porn, strippers, sugar babies, escorts, hookers, dommes—the categories and subcategories feel less like a list and more like an endless velvet labyrinth of sweat and nuance. It turns out, there are nearly as many ways to sell your own sexualized body as there are to have one.

Broadly speaking, sex workers include those who sell their bodies (and time) through sex, domination and submission play, and fantasy fulfillment for kinks that are eroticized in the minds of practitioners though not explicitly sexual in nature, such as spanking, feeding, etc. Sex work also includes those who sell an idea or image of their body and sexuality through strip clubs and other live performances, as well as porn, live webcam shows, and all the tiny corners of the internet where people are willing to pay to see something they have long craved and kept to themselves. It also encompasses a huge array of other experiences, because humans have a taste for sex that is vast and varied and delicious and strange, and sex workers cater to all of it.

To me, being a former sex worker often feels like being in a sorority built on grit and a hard-earned taste for fast money. Difficult, but undeniably fast. We, this sorority I imagine, are a heterogeneous riot of voices, less a community of women and more a network of cis women, trans women, and non-binary queers who perform a stylized version of womanhood for the gratification of clients—mostly cis, straight men of means. There are of course cis and trans men in the industry too, and non-binary people who performed a stylized boyhood. But throughout the world, 80% of prostitutes are women between the ages of 18 and 34, catering to men. So, many of us who have passed through this industry had girlhoods, and everyone who had a girlhood had that girlhood end. For most people I know, that end came with or around the realization that a woman's body is constantly judged, sexualized, and commodified. Sex work takes this commodification to its most literal point. Those who do it seek whatever empowerment can be found through it, however hard-won that empowerment is.

Sex work is not a monolith. Our experiences vary, as do our triumphs, traumas, and the amount of choice we actually have in this choice. We have burdens we share and burdens we don't, but we recognize this: we are people who at some point looked our own exploitation straight down the barrel, and made some money off it.

To be clear, we are discussing safe and uncoerced sex work, as uncoerced as any labor under capitalism can be. We are discussing the autonomous sale of intimacy, which is itself a complicated thought. Intimacy can take many forms, and it's surprising how many can be paid for in cash. Still, those who choose and continue to choose to stay in the adult industry know its violent edge. Most of this work is not legal. The field is overwhelmingly populated by gender and sexual minorities, and people of color often experience racialized aggression, bigotry, and financial injustice in addition to oppressions already at play. Sex work is also typically done by those who are economically disadvantaged, or by people who in some other way have their choices compromised by drug use or disability. Sex work can be dark. It can lead us to dark places and prompt reckless choices.

I have a few of these stories. I cannot trust that everyone will hear them the way I need them to be heard, so in my day-to-day life, I keep them to myself. I keep them, silent as a burning library set alight by someone else's hands. This is what most sex workers do. We shut our mouths and our legs and return to civilian life out of fear of being judged for what we have done. We have all heard the stories of jobs lost and families aghast. And so, we don't discuss the ways we have been damaged, just as we don't discuss the ways we have been enriched and bettered.

Because yes, there can be true rewards to this work, beyond just Instagramming yourself with piles of twenties. There can be a genuine tenderness in the performance of tenderness for the benefit of others. There is an exchange of unbalanced power, yes, but to me that exchange always felt less like a handshake and more like a complicated dance where the lead kept switching. There were clients who wanted words as much as touch. There were clients I came to genuinely care for, men who I (quite literally) whipped into shape, who I know I helped have more impassioned, honest, healthy sexual relationships with themselves and their partners. Generosity from other clients provided true and life-changing opportunities that would otherwise not have been open to me. Sex work taught me about myself. I do, on occasion, celebrate its memory.

We don't need to accept a life as a burning library. One way to stand in our power is to tell our stories. To tell as many individualized stories as possible, to give space and context to lives that are normally faceless and swinging in the public imagination between exotic and victimized. That is why a book like this one is necessary: to begin a conversation that centers, finally, on our own stories.

Clementine von Radics

naked on the internet
Vivienne L'Crave

i was naked on the internet before i had an email address
i won't get into all of that,
but i will tell you this—
i didn't have breasts yet.
and even if he asked,
though he didn't ask—
my yes could not
would not
have meant yes.

i used to wear all of my clothes at once.
i wanted all of the space between me and your gaze
to be filled with layers.
not like a suit of armor.
like a fucking minefield.
tensor bandage, under bra.
bra under camisole, under t-shirt.
under sweater under sweater under sweater.
and hunched all of the way over
all of the way down.
curving my spine until every vertebrae spiked out of my back
like barbed wire.
if you were going to touch me again,
it was going to leave a mark on you
this time
motherfucker.

sometime after then but before right now, we will call it the beginning
i fell in love with fashion, with music, with movement
through these things i learned how to relate to the world,
to make sense of the world
to turn up the volume and just let the world burn
when i needed it to.
the layers fell away and i got to know my very own skin.

it had grown thick with fear
and calloused with anger
and pale without purpose
and it did not look like me anymore.

it was peeling back and falling off
and something was shining underneath.
peeking out from the purge
it was my body.
it took some time for me to learn to navigate this—vessel of flesh
and corners
and curves
and wounds
and wonder
i wore my breasts like bullseyes and my hips like bullets.
i softened my skin,
i unfolded my shoulders, i raised my chin to the sky.
the sun drenched my flesh and i was golden again,
broken open again,
and i drank it all in
i unwrapped myself from this shroud of shame
that bound me to more guilt than any cadaver could carry.
i grieved for the innocence i lost.
and the years i spent blaming this body
for what happened to this body
before my lips learned to bend around the word
NO.

and then I danced.
right there on that bar top.
decorated in leather stretched over lace
red lips, fringe-hung hips
hints of skin soaked in sin
and a smile wide across my face.

i didn't know that power could grow back once it had been cut off
some people find freedom in string and some find it in cloth
mine was right here hidden underneath.
when i found it i waved it high above my head
and took pictures for the internet
for everyone to see
not for validation
but a declaration
you cannot,
will not
place shame on me
my naked skin
is not the patriarchy
my worth
is not measured by my lack of nudity
my value
is not calculated by adding or subtracting clothing
my power
is in my command for consent and respect
and i demand that you show it to me.

i am naked on the internet
and you don't get to decide
what that means.

Goddess, by *Magic of Light and Composition*

Baseball Metaphors

Zoey Morris

1.

I don't know a single thing about baseball
except that it's the Great American Pastime.
I figure, according to past experience,
bringing down a varnished wooden stick
over and over and over again onto
the base of a young girl's skull until
she can't remember her name
is also a true American Favorite.

2.

I don't know why:
    I sold pictures of my legs
    spreading like
    taking a (baseball bat)
Maybe. Just maybe. I figured:
    If I would be consumed /
    spat out / stomped through
    (tobacco plant) I might as well
    charge a handling fee and offer
    a delicately fingered personal touch.

3.

I charge cold cash
as I record myself
sitting on the edge
of my grandma's tub,
fingers slamming
(baseball bat)
flimsily in and out of my razor-burned pussy.
I moan a song called
"Take Me Out to the Ball Game"
but I'm not going to the field

and I sound more like
a whore.

4.
Dark lip: angry woman leaving marks on customer men I bite
Blue knee: sore woman my favorite color is aging bruises
Leg hair: messy woman I wish my legs belonged to me
Baseball hat: dyke woman pretends to love (baseball)
(Baseball bat): hit me harder through the television screen

5.
Intended audience is the only thing
differentiating the breaking of a body
from a ballgame for skinny little boys
You have two choices in this sort of situation.
You can either kick
as the (team) holds you down
they'll (homerun) you.
or you can quickly
chug (cracker jacks).
either way the (batter)
will (homerun)
all over you.

6.
I fall asleep
to the sound of
a man (batter).
the back of his
(jersey) says
[REDACTED]
and he is
(warming up)
to my voice,
through the
cable noise

of the phone
from across
the country.
he wants to
Slam
he wants to
Swing
he wants to
Bang
his (baseball bat)
20 bucks
strapped in
the pink halter
of my bra
(uniform)

7.
I hand the (baseball bat) to him.
I hand the (baseball bat) to her.
I hand the (baseball bat) to them.
I hand the (baseball bat) to you.

ORIGIN STORY FOR THE DAY SHE BECAME PROUD
Liv McKee

tar   spokesmen   plea   tame   pity sex
hack   floorboards   swallow   oil
absent tongue endure religion piper
wept   quiver   hail   bravado   nest

[or]

i made my way across the floorboards
and they did not creak. no pipers wept.
i left him there: business casual
       white-collar crime
                 the spokesmen—
it's not pity sex if you're paid for it.

you may say
that girl, swallow oil
that girl, absent tongue
that girl, a plea
but if i may,
i've endured religion far too long to be tame,
and i'm good at this. i left him there
                 made a deposit
weeded the marigolds
                 ate a sandwich
afternoon permission to be
full, not fill.

some days hack me in two, but a job is a job
and i am neither purity nor plunder,
and i still quiver,
still wax
    wane
           hail
with chosen lovers.
i spit out the work day,
slippery oil. spill. when i speak
it is a bite embrace. i reset, plush.
so if i may,
because indeed
i may
when i leave him there
he does not leave tar on me.
the floorboards do not creak.
i do not remember the spokesmen. it is bright. bravado
in my veins. this too, a nest.

THEY SAY A REGULAR PRACTICE OF AMBIDEXTERITY PREVENTS DEGENERATIVE BRAIN DISEASE
Liv McKee

so i brush my teeth with my left hand
step first with my left foot
backstroke first with my left arm, a windmill

post outcall with an aggressive client
who pinned me to the wall with too much tongue
told me he loved me and asked where i think our *tension* comes
from

after
i take myself out to dinner
place the chopsticks in my left hand
two taps
try to rewire the pathways in my arm,
cerebrum to fingertip like some sort of baptism
some spell of protection
a reset, a clearing,
a hope, even

though i must eat quite slowly to do so
though the rice grain spills
everywhere

DID YOU THINK WE WOULDN'T COME FOR YOU
for Stormy Daniels
Liv McKee

her cry for help the bullhorn of their hunt,
watch how she takes stock of your laughter
makes a dollar off your fear,
your respectability politics,
your husband's computer click
watch her rise
watch her take back the narrative of
breaking news:
sex worker pornstar files lawsuit against the 45th

her image now cliffjump
her name in the slandermouth of every boy who learned to fuck
from her photo
every woman with internalized misogyny for a tongue-cage
every congressman who has sought services

here's to Stormy, doing more for the "resistance"
than the DNC ever did,
sex worker political
sex worker unpraised deity

sex worker unpraised deity

sex worker unpraised deity

Vows of Virginity
Robin Gow

last night st. lucy came
to my door & knocked three times.
the mother the daughter
& the holy bedpost that i use
as a rosary.

running out of veneration,
she sat at my desk chair,
placing each scented candle of
her crown on the end table.
rose & cream & patchouli & lavender.

i asked her what she was
doing here so far from december
& she put a finger to my mouth.
her eyes looking up from the golden
plate, unblinking. white grape.
for broken vows
& pagan boys we never loved.
for the stained glass
on the brothel walls
we made a curtain. she told
me of bundles of wood
& fire that only women know.
she danced her fingers over flame to demonstrate.

i stuck out my tongue,
the taste of her ember as
sweet wine. eyeball in her
palm she fed me,
yes both eyes, off the plate.
juice down my neck,
across my collar bones.

she asked for my confessions,
turning them into pastries
on her plate. tea cakes
& macaroons. the powdered
sugar on our lips.

we will take this all
to the catacombs.
Diocletian, a statue outside
the window. he's dead now,
we know. but a man is
always a statue left somewhere.
i asked her if her
eyes would grow back
& already there
was another pair.
blue & lucid.

Temples of Venus
Robin Gow

st. afra smacked, pounding nails into wood
& i sleepwalked to where she stood in the yard;
her fishnet stockings, halo snapped into headband.

about a year ago i started touching myself again,
first just a fist overtop underwear,
mortar pestle me, i ground into sand, spilled

out my window. she's rebuilding the temples of venus
like the one where she used to be a hierodule.
a sacred sex slicer, a shrine shaking

slut like me. she says she can't believe
she ever sealed off her clit for god, for christ.
laughing, we make sacrifices to her,

the love goddess, chopping my dildos
sideways & pouring lubes into basins,
oh holy mother water. no ivory columns here,

just a treehouse. a ladder dangling
that i climb with my lover. we make sacred
our queer bodies. i show her how

i touch myself & st. afra dresses
us in fishnets, roses blooming where
we once had genitals, the scent of evergreen,

the altar where our blood comes out white.
myrtle's pollen pucker our throats, she prays
for us, that we find pleasure there.

Is Wednesday Your Real Name?
J. Random

The kind of girl who slips
right through your fingers
taking her time—fast enough
she goes down like regret, slow
enough you're used to the taste—
curvy and hard
to get over, not sweet
like the climax-collapse
at week's end, more satisfying
than the alarm clock prospect
of doing it all again
—middle of the road—
like her namesake,
so that when you're inside her,
you don't know
if you're coming
or going.

When Things Can't Fit

Davy Le Jones Nguyen

This is the kind of body
that does not seem terribly
feminine,
particularly for somebody
that believes in speaking it
into something more than a question mark.

This is the body that daytimes
As an occasional barista or boy or
ghost,
but that is because it can be a lazy body,
one that forgets to shave,
forgets to not wear baggy clothes
because I would rather be

swimming in myself
   than put something together

from a bunch of things
I don't always   understand.

I'm wishing instead
for something more like
an oversized god,

struggling to recognize itself,
struggling to not become
the kind of judge that condemned
Sisyphus to labor,
   or Prometheus to suffer
every day just like I would.

Rather, I wish for the body that is
more like the kind of god who is just tired.

This is the kind of body that
struggles to present itself,
because to present something this ramshackle
would be hoping that your body can become a gift,
become something you can hand over with a smile on
your face.

But it seems like this
asking for the world,
this requesting of a body
that betrays you less than a stranger
seems outlandish.

Because that is all I really want for myself.

For a world I can call my own,
and by world I mean,
    a body,
and by body I mean
something that doesn't fit
like a begrudging hand-me-down.

It can be the kind of thing to be grateful for,
grateful for having a body
that does not require any sort of unnecessary grieving,
a body that doesn't bleed out from itself   like a child's screaming,
scraped across the pavement underneath some shoe.

Rather,
it is the kind of body that picks itself up every morning,
remembers it can dance,
    however poorly, to that one song.

Sometimes life is like this
and you learn to sing in the silence,
dance through the pain,
a reminder that every hand-clap
can become some sort of hymnal embrace,

becomes the kind of chasm that closes,

the kind of close
that you only know when your
teeth fit together,
the kind of body
that learns to loan itself out
even if not all of it is returned and
        becomes the fiercest kind of laughter.

Hunting for Boise

Davy Le Jones Nguyen

It seems that many people have to hunt
for god,

and whenever they did,
it was mostly at night.

Fighting was always easier in the dark anyway.
I saw him first on Parkcenter Boulevard,
just before midnight
standing alone,
tall with tight hair made fine
and smooth enough for holding.

His face was softer than the soles of his feet,
and people called him pretty,
even if it was a sullen beauty,
and it only bothered him sometimes.

He preferred to have features
more like hammered steel,
more thin and sharp,
like razor blades
hidden away   in bowls of Halloween candy.

He pulled a bottle of whiskey from
his purse,
he shuddered
when he drank from it,
maybe he giggled too,
the way a child who
understands how easily
they can become ragdolled would giggle.

He offers the bottle and says,
        doesn't burn your throat much.
        Besides, if it did, then maybe people would listen.

I take a long pull and shudder as well.
I can't help myself.

The bottle slips back into the bag and as
quickly as he takes a drink, he says,
            one to make the body forget.
            two to make the forgetting feel more like my body.

Before long his phone rings
and he's off,

answering an invitation to
fly to heaven,
hoping this will bring
him one step closer to actually leaving.

God is mourning now,
unable to speak in clarity,
and whenever she does it is only in left-footed hymnals.

I wonder if there is song enough for him,
as he goes off,
wanting that body of shrapnel
to become   louder

than it already is.

I wonder,
if after all of this, there is still
a home to go to,
or if there is still a chance
for children to meet an embrace meant for a god.

I realize that's all they actually have.

He meets me in an hour,
at Wiseguy's,
like he said he would,
he's smiling at me a little bit,
he looks at a reflection of himself
as if everything far was suddenly close,
he says his name as if his body
has just become a sudden choir.

As we eat I notice his bag   again,
I ask him what he keeps in there,
              only things that children would regret
leaving behind.

Sex Work as Self-Immolation
Anonymous

It is as if I am a voyeur in my own body
Eavesdropping on grotesque mewls and exaggerated moans—
The slap of skin against skin, friction facilitated by sweat-slicked
flesh,
Resonating in the empty air—
As I flick my tongue over cracked lips
To allow for more noises I didn't know I could make to escape
them
... who are you? Why are you doing this?
But the version of myself writhing on a stranger's bed
Only responds by arching her back up, up,
As bedsheets spill through curled fingers, clenched fists

Maybe I'm just going through the motions, muscle memory
Or maybe the feeling of my mind, exiting through my pores,
Dissolving into thin air
Is more familiar than the sex itself
Maybe I find comfort in my slow descent
Down, down, until I am n o t h i n g
So that when I hit the bottom it won't hurt
Clearly it didn't hurt, you idiot, you didn't even notice
A certain sense of solace in the absence of real intimacy
In being used and discarded and in climbing off naked bodies,
Hauling myself onto the next one

Maybe, just maybe, /*like a hungry little whore*/ I fucking get off on that
But truth be told, I don't remember the last orgasm that wasn't faked
Or the last time that wasn't desperate, pleading, animalistic
Gasping oh my god yes, **fuck me** instead of **bury me**
So I give entry and I observe, a spectacle and a spectator all at once
In the hopes that one day I'll get lucky and it'll kill me,
Numb my brain until I'm so far gone that none of it will matter,
For it is so much easier to break completely…
… than it is to repair what will never be whole again

IN THE VIDEO YOU TOOK OF US FUCKING, THERE'S A MOMENT WHEN BOTH OF OUR GENDER TATTOOS ARE VISIBLE AND THAT'S HOW I KNOW JOY IS ITS OWN GOD

Vive L'oiseau

last night we counted backwards and realized at the same time
in each our own childhoods men's hands ate us before we knew
we looked like food / last night i bullied you into my mouth and
held you like a high note sliced thru an empty church / last night i
deer-flinched in the bright light and there is my back dipped into
your hands / there is our leg hair singing / this isn't about any
of that / i mean i want to hear how your name sounds on every
day / i want to drive you to the doctor / i want to photograph
awkwardly with you / i want to live too close to you to write
about distance / i think we don't fight because we don't want to / i
think we both don't believe we deserve it

To the One Who Told Me "Fuck off"
Christopher

To the one who told me "Fuck off,"
for any, whatever reason,
I won't be a target.
And I have to believe
there's a soul in there somewhere
but it ain't up to me
to dig it out.
So I'll dig the ocean
breathe the afternoon
park as close to the railing as I can
give my last fries to the gulls
watch the wind
push the waves in
and not waste another poem on you.

AFTER ANIMORPHS
Gigi Genet

I loved these books about children whose bodies
were continually destroyed in service

and knitted back again. They gave up skins
and limbs, spilled their insides endlessly,

but always shuddered back into
their baby-fatted forms. You saw

affectation in my mouth around
my fingers, but really I just gnaw

holes in myself to lay
on others. They close in

a marvel of regeneration and more
are torn or stretch open of their own

accord. All soreness is the same to the rallying
body. *You jaded little creature.* What else

am I to you? The best character
redlusted so terribly she even scared

herself. *You're like a baby
tiger with a bottle.* They saw

the width of space how cleansing how
unknowable its sundry stores of hurt

renewal. Crushed into bed I don't believe
in fresh skins. My body is the same

just bigger. *You like being brought back to infancy*
and weird memories. What animal

would you be? *A human.*
Sensations of stretching, alien

hands. Such radiant mutants.
The terror of morphing

was not that it hurt; only
that it didn't, that it should.

AUTHORISED PERSONNEL ONLY

TRESPASSERS BEWARE

Robin M. Eames

apocalypse glam
Robin M. Eames

At the end of the world the sun does not
turn black the seas do not turn red & the stars
do not fall out of heaven like shaken figs.
The bees are not disappearing. The air is loud
with the silence of trumpets. The oceans
swell with petrol & the sunsets are tainted
with a haze of hanging smog. At the end
of the world we lock our children in cages.
In Babylon sex workers on smoke breaks
watch the sky fill with scarlet dust & cry out
heartfelt orisons to Ishtar queen of whores
as fighter jets streak orange contrails overhead.
At the end of the world War Famine & Plague
ride forth without sword or scale or crown
& Death speaks quietly, without thunder.
Perhaps there will be survivors: Líf & Lífþrasir
whose names mean life & lover of life; Pyrrha
& Deucalion; Utnapishtim; Ziusudra; Noah;
Yu; Manu; Saoshyant; birds & turtles; snakes
& salamanders; devil fish; flowering plants.
Apocalypse derives from ἀποκάλυψις meaning
an uncovering / a disclosure / or a revelation
but at the end of the world we do not listen
to each other because we are all too busy
screaming; screaming because we are dying;
screaming because we are watching each
other die; screaming because we are hurting;
screaming because we are hurting each other.

The Siren Just Wants to Go Home Alone
RLynn

the old woman who owns the club/ comes to the stage/ says into
my ear/ "put your tips away/ make them think you're hungry"/
and then a man tells me where his wife is tonight/ where i could
be/ and so he sings a sound/ something like/ oh hunger/ oh
wanting/ and i/ i shake the chorus right in his face/ songbird
back to him/ oh the rhythm of a man/ who only knows how
to take/ and in the shower after my shift/ i solo to no one/
oh hardwood floors and glitter heels/ oh the stories i tell/ the
strength i find/ oh the ache of an always-singing throat

Late Nights & Lap Dances
Peace

I come to work with money on my mind
Lingerie on my body
And a plan for a man
With a bank account the length of my phone number

I find empowerment between my thong and six-inch stilettos
I choose this life and I don't feel guilty about it
Sex work
I don't actually have sex
But trust me it's a lot of hard work

Deciphering which misogynistic message is worth the most
money
Old white men are the best
I like to call it reparations

Maneuvering my way through the multitudes of men
Not finding myself on the wrong side of the wrong one
Each having his own motive
And me with only money on my mind
Which meant that my

Time needed to be
Spent
Ever so wise

Our security is pretty strict, "DON'T TOUCH THE DANCERS!"
But that don't stop men from working their creepy fingers up my
body
Me, remembering I chose this and
If I wanted to be a dick I could have you thrown out
But that would mess with my money
So I continue to straddle you, gyrating
Remembering when nights like these were spent at house parties
With a lil more clothing than I currently have on
But my pockets were light AS FUCK

It's midnight
Feet are sore
Heels creating an arch in my foot where there wasn't one before
There is still work to do
Money to be made
In this time my mother's saying
"Pain is beauty"
Actually applied

As I catch my breath . . .
Before scanning the room
Looking for my next prey
It felt good
To be the man
Or to use what I have to get what I want
Or to take what you have to get what I want
And you
Are my bitch!
Signed up for this
Making me feel less guilty when I take you for everything you
didn't plan on spending
Don't be a lazy stripper
Take pride in your craft
Use that body that momma gave you
Even when she don't know what you're gonna do with it.

The Day Shift
Jessica Barry

It's late March, and I'm driving to work in the slushy rain.

Where I live, we don't really have spring. It's winter for what seems like an eternity, and then it's summer. Spring is just a brief interlude where everything is covered in a layer of dust and grime.

The river, which divides the city into north and south, begins to defrost, overflowing its filth onto park pathways, forming stagnant pools that will provide breeding grounds for mosquitoes and threaten to flood the homes located on the riverbanks.

Even though I know it can't possibly be true, I imagine that all of the other cities in the world are experiencing hopefulness and rebirth right about now.

Flowers blooming. Grass turning green. Chickadees and bunnies flitting about.

And here I am, cursing the potholes and puddles of half-melted sandy snow that splash up onto my car, just so that I can spend my day sitting in a dark bar.

Suddenly, I hit what looks like a puddle, but turns out to be an ice patch. My car spins out of control and does a 180. Luckily there are no other cars around, but my heart is racing nonetheless. I pause, gripping the steering wheel with both hands, and take a deep breath before continuing on my bumpy journey.

"Stripper Dies in Car Crash." That could be a headline in a local paper on a slow news day if I died on my way to work.

But never mind that. I'm still alive, my car is alright, and I won't get fined for being late or missing work.

"What the hell are my tax dollars going towards?" I think to myself as I continue to navigate the dangerous terrain. The older I get, the more I'm starting to sound like my mother.

After successfully dodging the potholes, I finally arrive at Kisses to work my eight-hour day shift.

Ugh. I'm early.

I sit in my car and play games on my phone until exactly noon. I don't give them one more minute of my time than I'm required to. The only thing worse than being late for work is being early.

At noon, I start to drag the heavy black duffle bag that contains all of my stripper gear out of my dust-covered car, but the long strap gets caught on the emergency break and I fall to the ground. Great. Now my parka is dirty. I get up and brush off the dirty snow, unloop my bag, and approach the bar.

I pull back the heavy door to Kisses and walk into the darkness, waiting in the entrance a few seconds for my eyes to adjust.

There's no one here except the DJ, Mike, who is seated at his booth watching YouTube videos on his phone while eating spring rolls, and one bartender, Chrissy, who is reading a book and leaning up against the bar.

Barely looking up from his screen, Mike waves at me, and I wave back as I walk to the changing room behind the stage to don my uniform of white lingerie and stockings.

White is the WORST color. All of the dancers complain about it because it's unflattering on most people and gets dirty so easily. Maybe if they bothered to mop down the stages every once in a while we wouldn't have to worry so much about our costumes getting grubby.

The floor of the changeroom is covered in the same sandy layer that coats my car and my parka. A youngish-looking dancer I've never met before is sitting on a chair curling her long blond hair in front of the full-length mirror. She greets me and introduces herself as Janine.

"I'm Jessica. I've never met you before … how long have you been working?"

"Um, maybe like a month?"

"Ah, ok. Well, welcome to the shitty day shift at Kisses."

"Oh, I've done it once before. It's not so bad!" she says, laughing.

"Give it some time," I say.

After four years in the industry, I'm turning into a bitter lifer.

We don't say much else to each other the rest of the shift. The managers don't like it when the girls who are working the floor sit together and chat.

There aren't any customers right now, so I relax at a table near the back of the bar near the front entrance, while Janine positions herself at a table near the DJ booth.

Now we wait.

Several hours (and several levels up on Bejeweled) later, I see Garry walk in. He's a regular at Kisses, and is always good for at least one dance. Sometimes more if the DJ plays Metallica or Selena Gomez.

"Hi, Garry!" I say as he approaches me.

He's always pleased as punch when the dancers remember his name.

We exchange pleasantries before he finally says, "Well, let's get some dances then!"

After making our way to one of the private booths at the back of the club, he sits down in a ripped beige chair, and I close the curtain and step up onto the one-foot-high square platform in front of him.

Privacy is just an illusion, of course, since I know Mike is monitoring everything through the tiny cameras set up in the corners of the booth. Selena Gomez starts playing over the speakers. I guess Mike recognized Garry.

Sure enough, after the song ends, Garry pulls out another thirty dollars and places it on the little stage.

"Keep going," he says.

Every time I'm facing him I smile brightly, but whenever I turn around while dancing for him, my face goes blank. I do this with every customer. Gotta conserve my fake "happy" energy, even if it's just for a few moments.

When our time is up, I throw my robe on and step down from the platform. Garry grabs my hand, kisses it, and says, "Thank you, dear."

"Oh, you're welcome!" I say, beaming, even though I'm viscerally disgusted by the feeling of his moist lips against my skin.

I walk over to the DJ booth to give Mike the bar's cut of my money.

He marks two little ticks on a piece of paper under my name, where he keeps track of our private dance quotas.

I immediately head to the bathroom to wash my hands, rinsing away Garry's germs and the dirt from his money. Then I sit down in the same spot as before.

Play Bejeweled. Wait. Sell a dance. Wash hands. Repeat.

T4M
Cam

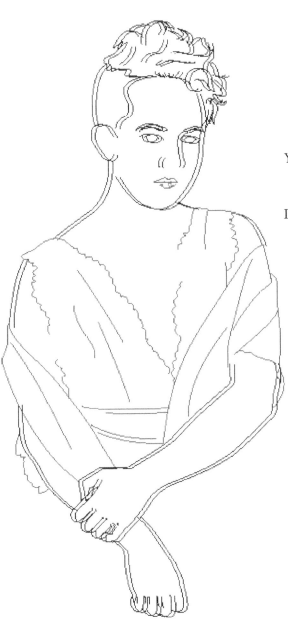

How hung are you?
Are you FTM?
Cleanshaven?
Got a pussy?
Tits? Size?
Rates?
BB?

You willing to go bare?

I want to   *feel*   you
I want to feel all of you

You want
You want
You want

I want

What do / want?

Ridden
Mateo Lara

> *they never know names*
> *and they never care to know*
> *here's $30, go home.*
Where do we go? 21. Down the street. All the flaws
of men in the abdomen. Where they stick—stick me
what does a queer boy know but bending over
make a whispering turn moan, a chant, another
groan on my thighs slick with wet, and his
eyes elsewhere.
> *All I ask is this:*
> *Do not harm me or kill me*
> *You may enter the soft, pink space.*

The Retiree
Kristy Lin Billuni

No way the woman scrutinizing Regina's resume would hire a girl with zero experience.

Regina studied the famed art dealer's immaculate, orange-painted lips and neat, auburn pixie cut. She admired the super-sleek Donna Karan skirt suit and the gallery's soaring, wood-beamed ceilings. She needed a steady job in art, this job, at the best gallery in the city.

So when those orange lips parted to release the words, "You're hired," Regina screamed inside. Back on track. Not that she'd strayed. Painting to meet deadlines had crushed her inner artist and left her burnt out. Take a break. Stock the fishing pond, she'd told herself.

Kay, a plain name for such a big deal, wore six-inch Louboutins that clacked on the polished concrete floor as she led Regina past an imposing series of lavender-and-black oil paintings. Her voice carried. "I'll call you with a start date as soon as I get your background check." She said it with rolling eyes and a mocking tone that trivialized the formality.

The words echoed through the gallery rooms and caught Regina by the throat. She could barely speak. Kay might as well have told her to forget it, that they only hired good girls, not girls like her.

Not whores.

She felt nauseous and dizzy, but managed to shake Kay's hand and let herself out onto the street. She stumbled around the corner in time to puke in the alley, away from the gallery windows. She had been naive to think she could land a straight gig so easily.

Inspired by an art model in a figure-drawing class, she'd tried posing naked. She found she relished the charcoal smeared not just on the palms of her hands but also the soles of her feet, felt freedom in all that exposed flesh.

After that, she tried escorting and dancing at gentlemen's clubs. She lucked out with a mentor who taught her where to stash money in her boots, how to add saliva to make lube last, and how to refuse the cliché that sex work ruined your life. It was saving hers, after all, arousing her sense of adventure, helping her see colors again. Besides, she told herself, she envisioned a career in the arts later, not politics.

She dabbled in porn acting and fetish modeling. Sometimes she found glamor, sometimes a gutter, but she loved exchanging sexual power for money, loved it so much she kept doing it for seven fast-paced years. Now she felt ready to make art again and leave the bachelor parties to girls like Bella.

"Three songs to start," she told Bella the next day at the diner. "One just to dance. Focus on the groom-to-be. Second song's a striptease, down to bikinis. Third's all girl-on-girl action, if you're cool with that."

"Totally."

"After that, it's lap dances and whipped cream. Write this down."

Bella dug in her handbag and found a blue greeting-card envelope. "This is for you." A cartoon fox rode a hot-air balloon through a purple sky with pink clouds that spelled out "Happy Retirement." She'd drawn eyelashes and lipstick on the fox. On the inside: "Sky's the limit now!"

Bella beamed at her. "What are you going to do next?"

"Open an art gallery." She wished she still believed in that dream. She couldn't even get a job in one.

"That's so cool." Bella rested her elbows on the table and gazed out at the diner parking lot. "Wonder what I'll be doing in seven years."

"Let's coordinate lap-dance prices. I usually start at fifty."

Bella put her hand on the blue envelope. "I'm gonna borrow this back, okay?" She took a pencil from the SuperLotto box beside the ketchup. "Fifty base price. That's for no touching?"

"Right. They want to get handsy? Fifty per tit—"

"What about below the waist?"

Regina left the lunch smiling. That silly card, Bella writing down her instructions, and daydreaming about her someday gallery almost made her forget she'd blown it. But for the next few days, she worried about a new retirement plan.

So the call from Kay surprised her. She picked up, determined she could at least give good phone. She rocked at phone sex, "fantasy making," they called it. One of her longest-standing callers coveted hours of dirty tongue twisters. *Pissy sissy's prissy pussy. Choosy coochies cherish chewy cookies.* It kept her sharp, filled her with ideas.

"Can you come by next Monday?" Kay said. "I open at eleven. Come at ten-to so we can chat first."

Not a word about hiring. Kay probably wanted Regina to "come by" before the gallery opened so she could call her a no-good, washed-up hooker and throw her out on the street.

Regina arrived at 10:49 the following Monday, dressed in her own Donna Karan suit and Louboutin heels. If Kay wanted to humiliate rather than hire her, at least she knew the dress code.

Kay sat on the edge of her enormous desk, talking on the phone. She held up one manicured fingertip. "Merci, Louis. Ciao!" She smiled at Regina.

"Kay, let me apologize." She launched into her rehearsed speech. Better to just confess. "I guess you know by now I wasn't completely…forthcoming in my resume."

Kay laughed. "If this is about your former career, you can stop right there. It's irrelevant, but I appreciate your honesty."

Regina blushed. "It showed up in the background check. I figured."

"Oh, please. That's just a credit score thing. Your resume gave you away. Just like mine did when I left the business. Photo stylist? Consultant? Customer service in Vegas? Give me a break."

Regina sat down on the desk next to her. "When you left?"

"Listen, Regina. We are everywhere." Kay draped an arm across Regina's shoulders. "So, how long were you in the business?"

Needs
Kristy Lin Billuni

One mirrored window shade rises, then another, a dozen of them ratcheting up—up—up with a ye-es—ye-es—ye-es, or down, a whoosh of rejection.

We dance on stilettos, daggers in pink shag carpet. I look at my reflection, not the man in the booth in front of me, and dread the moment when the other girls in this spinning disco ball detect that I am not beautiful or cool enough to work at their peep show. In my fairytale-sisters-fight fantasy, they expose me, tear away jewels, rip hunks of flesh, snatch fistfuls of hair. Blood dribbles from acrylic nails.

My attention slips, allowing brief contact. He has been waiting five minutes for me to make this mistake. Though he does not stop jerking off, he does align every one of his teeth to smile at me. His comment splatters all over the glass. The shade drops.

seducing god
Mason

My prayers sound a lot like "God, if you want my time, here is my hourly rate"

My body is baptized in bills

My amen tastes a lot like the loneliness of men with just enough money for me

The Bible and dirty talk intertwine in the ears of men who pay me to forget the difference

Communion is cumming and cumming is communion

I'll tolerate the holy ghost of a man's love if money is in my hand

My sins and Sunday scriptures are the same list of lines I use to tell men to pay me or fuck off

God's grace and cigarettes after sex both feel like money in my pocket

I have not given up on God

I confess like "oh Jesus Christ yes" and "oh God more" to a man who's ordained as daddy as long as his wallet is out

A hotel room in lingerie and church in my Sunday best are synonymous, they start with "oh God" and end with cash, whispering "thank you"s

is there any way to say i love you when i don't
Mason

if i said thank you/and i meant it/if i said thank you/and i meant i'm sorry/ would you say you're welcome?

if i said i'm sorry/i'm sorry/i'm sorry/i'm sorry/and i meant it/ if i said i'm sorry/and i meant goodbye/would you say it's okay/ would you say i forgive you/

would there be anything to forgive?

if i said goodbye/and i meant it/if i said goodbye/and i meant forever/would you say the i love you too that should have been there/

would you say i love you again, in case i just didn't hear it right?

when you whisper i love you/is there any way i could pretend i didn't hear a thing/is there any way i could pretend i love you too? is there any way to say anything else because i am not ready to say goodbye just yet/

but i'm at a loss for words/

Thigh Boy
Mason

My thighs

You run your hands across them, call them home, learn their curves and their creases and their scars and their lines, you poke ink into the skin and teach my thighs how to take something foreign and make it their own.

What am I supposed to do with my thighs?

My lips

You press yours against mine and teach them how to say your name, teach them to whisper sweet nothings and say I love you; you cannot teach them how to love. But you teach them to say I love you anyways.

What are my lips supposed to do with me?

My hands

You read my palms like a book without an alphabet, you use no guide, you don't look at any of their lines; you tell their story on your body, introduce them to each other, show them how good they feel connected in prayer, especially when they don't believe in a god.

What are my hands supposed to do with each other?

My body

Is learning.

This is Our Prayer
Ben Jorisch

All my friends are drug addicts.
They stole my good silverware.
But it doesn't matter
because we'll all soon be dead.

All the so-so minds of my generation
slinked back, opted out, devoured by
a host of venoms
revived by paramedic
not even given the luxury to die.

And the best of us
dead or in jail
for burning for a little more
than the fire
and never sleeping to dream
only dreaming to sleep.

But what we have suffered here
is the end of that
and soon we'll join
our better angels
whose departures put aches in our bones
and grew us old in an evening.

And the world gone by
as though it were nothing
as though we had something more
than the seeds we sowed
but how could we plant
when our hearts were
deforested.

Our eyes have seen too much
let us see no more
protect us from
ourselves
we never meant any harm
everyone else that we hurt
just got caught up
in our destructive momentum

SMOKE WITH ME
Anna Suarez

I smoke a cigarette before I kiss you.

Do you care if I smoke?

No, as long as you share it with me.

I am a sex worker. I am a secret smoker.

My biggest relief is the cigarette after I leave a townhouse, a hotel room, a house on a hill, a bar, a restaurant . . .

But *you* kiss me outside Scooter's, cigarette in your hand. You interrupt my drunken monologues with your lips. I am not angry. The magnetism is too much.

Can I sleep in your bed? I just want you next to me.

In dreams, we sway to each other's snores. In the morning, we fuck.

April. I am smoking next to you. There are cherry blossom trees blooming beside the view of the parking lot. We ash our cigarettes in empty beer cans.

In the morning, we smoke together. After sex. After the spinach mushroom scrambles. Wrapped in blankets, you pass back the Marlboro 27.

I sit on the toilet, pressing on my abdomen; I mourn the droplets escaping. I wish I could keep them here.

I am a hummingbird when you open the door. Your bike spandex under a pair of shorts, I have never tasted anything like this.

I call you Papi.

A text from you arrives and I cancel a booking. You open the door and I cancel another.

You leave again. You come back. You leave again.

I am a sex worker, fingers cramping from devotion.

You come back and I am a hummingbird again. I quit smoking.
My mouth tastes sweeter for you.

My identity—a sex worker or a former sex worker—shrivels as I
push it away to be close to you.

I'll be your mistress if I have to, *soy todo tuyo.*

The moonlight reveals her. You touched her. She is softer
and sane.

In the light you return, my wings break. We smoke a cigarette.
Ash reveals the secrets behind your lips.

Yet, I love you. I try to fly to you, but there are no flowers your
way. We weaken. Our cigarette does not taste the same.

I am a sex worker, knees burning from the squall of betrayal.

I light a cigarette.

Margaretha

J. Mork

There is always that moment when I'm caught being dyslexic at work. Neither my plump juicy ass nor my lush red hair distracts from the fact that I cannot count coherently past 15.

"Count your punishment spankings," says Golfer Prime, a client I love subbing to. I get to about 10 before I start skipping numbers because they all seem to be the same sounds. Golfer Prime's prime concern is the specific order. The order seems to be everyone else's top concern while topping me, despite the fact that numbers are only representations of the physical strikes. But no matter what words we use to represent the strikes, I am still struck that many times. When every director barked, "Zoe—learn your lines," I realized that traditional theater did not hold a place for the low-memory and neuro-diverse individual. Though my hopes of acting quickly faded, the makeup, costumes, and drama still beat wild in my heart of desire.

I left the straight job world at 26. It wasn't into me either, so it was a rather mutual decision. I see now that one of the first indications of my life trajectory was the character I chose to enact for my Catholic theater class: Margaretha, better known as Mati Hari. The books and articles all pegged her as a spy, yet alluded to her trading sexual favors for indelicately tasty information. I received an "A" on that project and soliloquy, partly because I fantasized about her for hours. Was I the torturer? Was I being tortured? Excited by either outcome, I often came to orgasm during this solo soliloquy practice.

In school, the grammar was idealized, never the content. Toward my 10th year as a ceramics student, I found a new strategy to fit into the mold and complete my assigned papers: I created dinner and clean laundry, and a peer created my paper.

During college, I was a nanny for a soul-sucking family. Those long, low-paid hours gave me ample opportunity to consider the content of my Women's Studies classes and world experience. I began to contemplate what it meant to be a good woman. I saw that my caregiving patience and creativity was certainly being capitalistically abused at seven dollars an hour.

I read *Macho Sluts* and *Stone Butch Blues* and saw reflections of a life I wanted to live. Then, on a Thursday in October 1997, I went to an interview at a local dungeon. I filled out an application, scattering information throughout the confusing boxes, but the interviewer took one look at my stature and asked me to come back on Wednesday to work with another woman who would show me the ropes—as well as the clips, paddles, and cleaning routines.

The next day, I quit my nanny job. I was sitting on a bench in Noe Valley with the jerk husband, watching his child bully another child on the playground.

"Could I call you to babysit when we go out to dinner or to Hawaii for a vacation?"

"I can't," I said. "I'm going to be working nights. I'm becoming a dominatrix." I got up to go to my car and they never called me for childcare again. I left them to their messy family life.

My first session took place the following Wednesday. The excitement of the unknown, the hair and makeup, the feeling of being needed, the acting and reacting with no offstage asshole yelling, "Zoe, learn your lines!" I collected $40 for 30 minutes of topping.

Maybe this is what I was supposed to do all along.

As a child growing up in Germany, I had learned all the feminine rules cross-culturally and developed very modern European sensibilities about nudity and sexual mores. This upbringing created a whole new way for my brain to see numbers when school shuffled me into all those special needs math classes. I had travelled the world at 12, and I could change money in my head from Deutsche Marks to dollars. I could multiply for black market denominations of money exchanged hurriedly and under stress in tourist hotels in Egypt, Czechoslovakia, and East Germany.

Even now, I think of numbers not by their names, but as blocks that fit together, like Tetris. This system works perfectly with fractions of hours and bundles of money or time…yet I have never passed pre-algebra.

In the workplace I have created for myself, I am in charge. My success stems from being organized around time, space, kink, and the emotional temperature of my beloved clients. I remember each person's emotional resonance and the emotional wave they leave in my mind. The logistical minutiae of meeting places and legal names will never pass my lips, as I cannot remember them. My brain tests out to 3% short-term memory, and I don't see this changing.

Here are the things I do remember at the end of my work hours: I want to travel. I want to know new people. I want different experiences than are offered to most women in the United States.

This is the special gift that my neurodivergent brain brings me: the ability to feel the energy of new people. I remember old clients and what good feelings we had between us. I am never bored if they want to do the same thing as last time, because I may not even remember the details. "I am excited to be in this situation again, with you," I can tell them truthfully.

I might not have been so far off as a high schooler reenacting Margaretha. I was going to be a theatrical professional, just not a spy who had to remember specific information. Although I was definitely suited for the torture and being tortured part—unlike Margaretha, who was shot by the firing squad.

Music to Watch Boys to

Lux Aeterna

I got that summertime, summertime
sadness siren calls us through the speakers
in the locker room and we are laughing
It's early by our standards; we are late
The girls are curling or straightening,
applying false smiles and false eyelashes
Amping each other up for our shift, kissing
cheeks and swapping breaths, helping
mirror checks before strutting out
swilling and selling

We are shrieking our banshee laughter
for every small death that comes
tonight

Melissa uses her real name on stage
but the remix cues her better than the DJ

We say it's *her song* like it belongs to her
We mean she belongs to it, to the music
to the drum tattoo that designs her heartbeat
Makes her larger than life, makes her glory
Makes her the closest thing to goddess
so you want to reach out and touch
her divinity

I'm told the Hebrew word *kedeshah* means
both prostitute and prophetess

One by one we leave the lockers after
we have belladonna'd our eyes fuller with
looking-for-you-yes-you-always-you

You with your _____ hair
your _____ smile your _____ shirt
your _____ hands your _____ taste in _____
You with your wallet

Fill in the blanks in time to the bass line

There is something to love in everyone
We know that or we wouldn't do this
Couldn't do this
job

Fine China

Lux Aeterna

The girls wanted to name her Charity
but she already knew not to put your shoes
on the counter or your purse on the floor

The men said she had skin like fine china
and I bet they dreamed of breaking her
open wide over their king beds

She had long black hair and a milk pitcher
face holding Sunday morning sweet cream
but her tongue was a steak knife

She named herself Steele
as she stood towering five foot four
in locker room six-inch stilettos

Sharpening the blades in her mouth
on her whetstone phone, her unsmiling
serrated laughter cut the call short

A lie everyone who hasn't worked a club
believes is true: We always have enough money
All of your bankrolls are ours

Even fiancés can believe that

Steele was their support-beam structure
even as he said, *Baby, you have easy money—
what does it matter?* relaxed on the couch

that she paid for after his third lost job
due to a "Lack of Application"
before he applied himself to another woman

Steele set fire to their building, let it snow ash
keeping only the strong frame of her standing
Rent finally feeling easy as an accusation

And just as she finished decorating her own
space with common luxuries, he calls her name
Says it like a secret spare key to the building

that's long since collapsed

So when she hangs up, she only looks fine china;
she chose the name she gave herself here to feel
unbreakable. She says to her squatter,

I will no longer be taken advantage of—
not by you or anyone

Television Heaven
Lux Aeterna

What's your real name?

That is *my real name,* she says
and she would prove her license
except she wouldn't dare

What's your real name? he asks
like a lawyer at interrogation
after she insists again it's real

She gives up, says
Annie or *Maria* or *Nicole*
or anything to shut him up

as he says his name is
Don Juan or *Casanova* or *Big* G
She doesn't care what his name is

as long as he comes when she calls

As long as it's a pseudonym
for Rainmaker

and then after he makes it rain
he asks for her number

Would you think to take a waitress home
with your paper-bag leftovers? Well
maybe you would

But he's a Rainmaker
so she gives him her area code
like signing up for the weather channel

and he asks,
What's your real number?

That is my real number, she says
Only it isn't: it's a forward mask
because she wouldn't dare

She's seen your television heaven

We all know the programs that programmed you
to say, to want, to take, to have, to do

Wolf in sheep's skin or a pack
of sheep is still more than one of me

You are dangerous

We all know the questions to ask the clubs
when we audition them like they audition us
and we're listening for the safe word

Your television heaven plays, pauses, repeats
but on every one of our screens is a clip
in black-and-white of us just doing our jobs
Going through the motions in time with the music

—and we think of it without the music

Playing, pausing, repeating before
the seven-day forecast predicts more rain
An official news voice says something
that translates to *asking for it* dead
calm discussing a cadaver in a trunk
without any hint of surprise
as he says her real name
flat as an allegation

Gods & Monsters
Lux Aeterna

Nothing about this work is
easy

Not a rock-and-a-hard-place situation
Even if some of us are light as feathers
others are made stiff as boards, robbed
of choice and *that* cannot be forgotten

Not the pole bruises on our ribs
our thighs that we have to explain
to sterile doctors while also sure
to thank them for their concern:
another girl will need it

Not the lack of salary, making only
what cash you bounce off our asses
We know what it is to work for a buck
but also what luck feels like when
half a night is an entire month's rent

You know you're a stripper when
you've held a girl in the locker room:
Someone gave her a ripped-in-half dollar
or threw their moist pocket change at her
Someone stole her bag and all her money
then showed up to her house uninvited
Someone told her no one could love her
little girl lost too long to the woods

But those are strange full-moon nights
for werewolf men;

Our comeback is a pack howl
for the girl killing it on stage
a whole Yellowstone Park of us:
ow ow owouuuuuuu!

And she shines like the moon

This is our territory. We held her
while she was inhaling cigarettes
until they became her, smoldering
unsure if she could live this, then
saw her send signals in the smoke
Claimed herself out of an inferno
fanned her own flame into a bonfire
learned she was always burning
embers bright inside herself

Her existence is an act of loving

and that sets us to sparking

We take up her torch song
Our salt sweat burns into colors
and we are the flare that beckons
Flickering, dancing, remembering
the parts of us that are incandescent
We can never be put out, we are
transcendent

We know how to change fear
of the dark into a blaze
healing after hearing
society screaming,
> *You're strung out, drugged out*
> *You dropout, you fuck toy*
> *What did Daddy do to you*
> *You should be ashamed*
> *You're worthless*

—We know we can do this
Everything we ever had, we pried out of palms
using white smiles full of sharp teeth, everything
we ever had was never a handout

We are incendiary
You can't shame us

Nothing about us is
easy

Honey, I'm on fire
I feel it everywhere
Nothing scares me anymore

EBONY PRETENDS NOT TO UNDERSTAND SAMBO (EVEN THOUGH SHE LIVES WITH THE PLANTER'S WIFE)

Christina Springer

Civil War Reenactment,
circa 2002, she binds.
Wrists to antique
canopy bed. Turns up oil

lamp. Folds muslin skirt
to leave no telltale
wrinkles or marks. Pins
petticoats to bloomers,

carefully pushes too deep.
Adorns. Bejewels me
in my blood. Drops
the ass flap; caresses

quivering flesh;
smacks hard. Laughs.
She yanks my laces.
Taffeta stretches tighter.

Whalebone forces
my brown shell upright;
She does not care
to break spine or skin.

Leaves me breathless
enough to barely stay
conscious. On the wall,

octoroon daguerreotypes
recall marrow-deep
perversion. Eyes accuse,

You let
her tie you up?
You let
her beat you?

Yes, Mistress,
I whisper. She whips
me until I crack. Peak.
Fold into a golden meringue

she eats slowly every time
we play the peculiar game.

EBONY EXPOUNDS ON CULTURAL SHIFTS REGARDING PERCEPTIONS OF BEAUTY AND FEMALE BODY IMAGE AS DEMONSTRATED BY THE CASTING, BLOCKING, & PIVOTAL PLOT DEVELOPMENTS FOR PORN ACTRESSES

Christina Springer

1935

Lily lesbians
frolic, thump.

Clumsy. Joy
seeking.

Silly girls
piano each other.

Silent lips
chattering

ragtime
giggles.

They pout.
Act goofy,

genuine.
Squeeze

eyes tight.
Guide each other

into the frontier.
Fresh, fleshy

bodies. Untried
moving pictures.

1950

He begins flaccid,
it takes a lot of time
for her to harden him.

His eyes lovingly
caress her heavy hips,
hairy pudenda, arms, and calves.

He strokes her head.
Teases her nipples,
gently, like a real

husband would touch
his wife in a modest
hardworking bedroom.

1975

White hippies,
psychedelic room.

Two women,
a man befuddled

by his extraordinary luck.
And now what? Should he

kiss the true blonde
(fluffy v-shaped proof)

or stoke the brunette's breasts
(thick forested armpit valleys)

His face contorts with confusion
rather than pleasure.

Honest desire.
He wavers.

Looks at each woman.
Immobilized with concern

about pleasing
both. Peace. Love.

Tuning out. Being in
two grooves at once.

2001

Fake breasts,
Shaved mounds.

Two platinum service
a man in stark raving color

as he stares off into space,
closes his eyes,

never touching the women
with anything but his cock.

CHARLIE COMPLIMENTS EBONY

Christina Springer

Sugar nigger lips,
pretty pouting

dick suckers.
Your women

were made
for pole greasing.

Pillows begging
for somebody to fluff

plump them.
But, curve

me a Jet beauty
smile. Honey,

blow me
a kiss,

before I churn
fat out of those buttery

Negress kiss biscuits.
Smear you with my super

special creamy
beauty lotion.

AT HOME, EBONY PREFERS FISTING

Christina Springer

Near death
or dream.
A door. Tunnel
widens. One finger

beckons in front
of cervix like angels
singing, *Stay.*
Stay! Hips sigh.
Parted. Deep

dusk breaths.
Two
fingers spread.
Knead.
Thrust need.
Sweat like resting
dough. Spine
rising.

Three, thrust. The first
orgasm—oven-hot
swimming heat
haze. Legs spill
over shoulders.
Rising. Four,
oiled fingers

sizzle. Back
brown loaf arched.
Now. Five curl.
Clench. Break
like bread promises.

Relax to rhythmic
tender punching
passion. Vulnerability
at arm's length.

PYRENE*

Christina Springer

Whores will not be
kept from the safety

of your comfort.
Before Alexander

salted, women
poured secrets.

Scorn-filled
huddle. High

tide eyes diminished
my shores. Good

women begrudged
me their extra seed

and clean water
drawn in daylight

hours. Alexander pierced
the city's tender

skin. All life
holes salted,

ravaged. I rose.
Spit in his face.

No one knew
I hoarded

my harvests
for your protection.

*After Alexander the Great destroyed the fortifications around Thebes,
Pyrene, a famous prostitute, offered to rebuild the city walls at her own
expense. Her only condition was that they erect a plaque that read,
"Destroyed by Alexander and Reconstructed by Pyrene the Prostitute."

Reluctance

June Sayers

I shudder as the man sitting across the table from me rises to use the restroom. I down the rest of my wine to calm myself.

I shouldn't worry. He's leaned closer to me at every story I've told about my wild college days. He's laughed whenever I've joked about my roommate who's ignorant of how I make money. He's wrapped his hand around mine, cradling my palm, before saying, "I'm surprised to meet a girl who knows about luxury car brands."

I extract my phone from my patent leather purse. I reread the messages in which he fawned over my legs, my ass, my svelte figure, all of which I've displayed in my shortest black dress. I recall the topics he's mentioned but that I haven't raised: his interest in magical realist literature, his love of South Asian cuisine, his Jaguar that he wants to exchange for a Bugatti.

Of course, among these messages is the one that scares me. He wrote about this being his "first time" with a woman like me. Although he was "ready and willing," this was "new ground." Words like these jeopardize payment. Words like these lead to the lamentations I've memorized.

"I like girls who are more traditional."

"I'm not really into that."

"You're just not what I expected."

Fortunately for me, this man returns to the table. He wants to continue to evaluate my gestures, assess my voice, estimate my price.

Within moments, the waiter begins fawning over this man of evident status. He lists wines that I couldn't afford after meeting 10 clients. The man across from me smiles or winces at all the names he recognizes.

Now asked about our wine, he opens his mouth, closes it, and then stares at me. This man who has ordered for girls who are more traditional hesitates with me. Although his deviation distresses me, when on the stage, the actress can't display those foreign emotions. I nod my assent quickly.

"I'll have another glass of the Clos du Marquis, and the lady will have another glass of the Morgeot." The obsequious waiter praises his astute tastes before departing. The man across from me speaks.

"When I was walking back, I noticed *The Wind-Up Bird Chronicle* sticking out of your bag." This feels more like a test than a question. He wants to see if I'm a demure coquette or a brutish ogre. He wants to test-drive me the same way he would the new Bugatti.

"It's my second time with it," I say. "I love it, but I think I like 1Q84 better, even if doesn't show off Murakami's skills as a postmodernist. Then again, I prefer Murakami at his most standard and sincere. I don't want him to be Pynchon."

"Now there's a name I haven't heard in ages."

I nod while he rants about *Gravity's Rainbow*. I agree with his assertions about the book: it's long, it's meandering, it's intentionally inaccessible.

His earlier messages said he'd use our conversation to see if he could be intimate with a girl like me or if he's not really into that. If he won't pay me unless we have this connection, then I need to discuss the topics I know.

"You said you were more into the magical realists anyway, right?"

"More Salman Rushdie than the McOndo school."

"So, you disagree with Gene Wolfe that magical realism is fantasy written by people who speak Spanish?"

Which, of course, engenders a discussion about the historiography of the British Empire that lasts until we finish our next glasses of wine.

I tell him I don't need another when our waiter comes with the check. He pays it, rises, and approaches me. As he does, his sinewy arm hovers behind my lower back, right where my skin ends and the satiny fabric of my dress begins.

"Is everything all right?" Although I don't want to ask this question, I can't refrain. I need this answer that he's never had to give to another girl. I need this answer before he's naked and lying on top of me. I need this answer before he reconsiders, decides it's not right, and strangles my neck and his mistake.

He answers with a faint nod. I place his hand on my back so he can lead me out of the restaurant.

This is where he balks. This is where he sticks with the Jaguar and doesn't buy this strange, new, exotic car that he's tried.

"This night has been . . . unique."

I shiver. Unique means outlandish, ridiculous, a story during which his friends spit out their beer while laughing.

The road is silent behind me. No cabs approach, and he doesn't raise his hand to hail one. I can't ask him to elaborate. I can only repeat his statement as a question.

"Unique?"

"Of course," he says. "My friends always tell me to shut up when I talk pretentious literature. But you know more about it than me. You're dropping Gene Wolfe quotes, bringing up Murakami's postmodernism, and I had no idea you'd read—"

"Wait," I interrupt, "So, to make sure, you don't have a problem with me being trans?" He shakes his head while smirking.

"That? God no." Now his hand stretches over the cracking, painted void. "I was fine with that the moment I saw what you looked like in person."

A yellow beacon shines around the corner.

"No, what surprised me was you talking postmodern literature. That's the first time I've done that with a girl. And a girl doing this job, no less." He shakes his head as if marveling at the size of the Earth relative to the galaxy. After he's opened the door for me, I wait until we're both inside the cab before speaking.

"Well, I hope it's not a bad thing that I liked *Gravity's Rainbow* enough to reread it."

"Not bad at all," he chuckles. "Just not what I expected."

Latex & Lube
Kay Kassirer

my sexuality moonlights as mistress
dresses up as girl next door
cloaks itself in fantasy

my sexuality has an hourly rate
charges extra for choking
only has sex with people it does not love

my sexuality looks like crisp bills in candlelight
like envelopes full of fifties stuffed in underwear drawer
like pictures with my face blurred but my tits out

my sexuality smells like scented candles and stale semen
tastes like latex and lube
looks like anyone but myself

my sexuality hides behind lingerie and white wine
says no   quietly
followed by
          thank you
followed by
          sorry

my sexuality tried to fit itself into a box
but now Schrödinger is not sure if it is alive anymore

my sexuality is fisting the system
is fucking the patriarchy
is forgetting last night ever happened

my sexuality looks like memories I can't erase
and money that doesn't feel like mine
and strangers and their fucking expectations

my sexuality knows what it looks like
wants to tattoo whore on its inner lip
so when you spit that word at it
we'll both know it was in its mouth first

my sexuality wears dyke like a tattoo it sometimes lies about the
meaning of
but regardless it is always on its skin

my sexuality gets shy when trying new things
expects others to expect it to be experienced

my sexuality is experienced
and by that I mean often experiences its body not feeling like it's own

my sexuality had forgotten the direction of home
but then found love bright as north star
found comfort in the crook of their arms

found partners that hold me after a long day at work
don't judge me when I show them where it hurts

my sexuality used to be strictly a performance
outfit put on for the show
costume taken off when curtains close

my sexuality is reinventing its boundaries
relearning it's confidence
remembering a time before it only existed
as a mirror reflecting someone else's desires

my sexuality says no
without saying
thank you
without saying
sorry

Work Follows Me Home
Kay Kassirer

when I say my work follows me home
what I mean is
most nights
I don't know the difference between sex and acting

but once,
a lover kissed me so hard and soft at the same time
that my hands started singing their name

I mean,
they didn't have to touch me to hold me

I mean,
they were able to hold all of these broken shards without getting
cut

TERMINAL
Julia Laxer

Flights of fancy, take your pick—

seats are expensive.

This window can only get

so
close.

Eyes scanning the runway
…looking for passengers

staying
too long.

>   *Why did I bother with the transient ones?*

> The clubs
> near nothing
> and no one

>   but leavers?

>   I always had
>   one foot out
>   the door—

—the other one,
     tethered.

To a wing.
Or a heel.

Made of cash, feathers,
and smelling

        of paradise.

CABARET
Julia Laxer

503 West Burnside
Street Portland, OR 97209

On the corner in Chinatown, I fall off the stage…

Pink-eye stinky
basement locker-rooms
shared with the kitchen.

Prepping onions. Sour Ranch. Stale scents. Cycles.
Shitting with the door open. Blooms of baby powder. Hair spray.

Victoria's Secret everything—as if glitter could cure us.

Stage lights made marks caused by birth disappear.
Crevices caused by the knife—bruises—fists.

All faded in the roselight.

Now, this room is empty.
A lock. No key.

Paper cranes fly, where I once fell.
Moons. Suns. Moons. Suns.

Swerving over the lines.

Bruises ghost my arms and my hips sag
with the impact of the bar
and the brass pole around the cage.

I know there is glass, still in my foot.
I know my eye is still pink from the red lights.

Missing the baby-oiled dancers
and the needing and the needing and the needing.

Missing the needing on the corner of 503 West Burnside Street…

And the glitter.

Sweetie
Julia Laxer

I have all the theories.
I wear more lipstick.
I forget my lips.

> Being honest about lovers and lips,
> even though I've lost them.

> Even if
> I've lost them.

Have I eaten today?

> I'm not keeping count.
> Yes, but I'm not lying though ...

A woman strokes her hair.
One time I ate an orange.

> My throat constricts
> with juice of orange segments.

Actually, it was a tangerine ...

> No.

It was a mandarin.

It's happening now.
I choked, then.

Something hard.
Something ready.

Something ready to choke or maim me.

Pleasure.

In that
sunset

we could   have had.
If only   you stayed

—longer

Daddy's Girl
Julia Laxer

wait it out

hun

cuffing season

only lasts

til the cherries

bloom

An Ode to Subculture Club
Strawberry

Waiting in the parking lot, decked out, humming
Everyone rolls up
Hugs and shouts and shots and love
It's Saturday night and we are a cavalry, a riot, an orgy of spikes
and nicotine and home

When someone who hurt me shows up
I duck inside
my wife, my best friend
my idol, the headliner
Follow
They hold space while I hyperventilate
They say, your call comrade
And it is, it is

I go to the sound booth, talk shit, rally strength
It's your call comrade, they tell me and
I stay, fuck him, it's my scene
I clock him in the pit
I fall in love
I spit and kiss and throw elbows and get lost
Tinnitus and bruises
Solidarity and back up
Point em out stomp em out
My man mingling with one of my clients
My heart beating out of my chest
But fuck, who cares
I am strong and so loved
A hundred hands at my back
Smiling mouths
Dead serious

We walk to logan's in the morning
Run into punx
Eagles flying high and
Everything is perfect

Today I'll help a baby sex worker
Post his first ad
Flash photos and acronyms
I have his back
It's his call comrade
And it is
It is

One Day
Strawberry

I am thinking of quitting/ no more thousand-dollar days, in a daze
of oily fingerprints, slithering in and out of lace panties/
How do you quiet a siren's song? How do you buff out the sly glint
in your eyes?
When I am touched by someone that likes me for me, my breath
quickens, heart stutter steps/ urgent
lips, fast hands in my hair, pulling, holding, exploring/ I fear I may
turn to liquid lust and it turns me
on/
At work when touched, I am hard plastic, recycled. I am elsewhere,
anywhere elsewhere/
That emptiness can't be good/ for me or him/
To my lovers, I don't ever want to be icy/ removed/ sterile/ but how
do you remove a mask fused to
your face?
I don't want my body to feel like some vague fleshy thing/
I want electric current gasp giggle stretch—
I was thinking of quitting/
On a bad day, when the money is never enough
When there is no glamour, just pubes in your teeth and too many
cigarettes/
I itch, scratch, squirm, angrily waiting for my phone to light up/
"U avail?" "babe?"
I sigh, sift listlessly through 20s and 50s
I text back,
"Yeah,"
I gave up on quitting/
Realizing freedom/ autonomy/ control/ security/
Would not be handed to me in any other workplace/
Not my grubby, trans, tatted body
Nor my soft, furious, depressive, insolent heart/ brain/ soul
I flick ash into the gutter, yanking up thigh-highs and texting my wife/
One day,
I'll quit

A Whore's Prayer
Strawberry

Let him be clean
And easy to please
Let him leave
When his time is up
And leave a good review
Or at least
Not a bad one

Let the money come
Easy and
When convenient
Or at least
When I'm awake

Let my body be safe
Unharmed at the end of the hour
Blood still surely pumping
Eyes still seeing sharp

Let my name be
Untarnished
Synonymous with sweet and wholesome things
Let my secret be safe
Or at least
Understood

About the Editor

Kay Kassirer (they/them) is a poet, activist, youth advocate, and community organizer. They have been a full-time sex worker since 2015, after being relieved from their previous job for having "too many panic attacks". They have toured internationally with the chapbooks *Confessions of a Queer* and *Unbandage the Wounds*, and have earned their place on several competitive final stages— notably the Capturing Fire International Queer Slam (2016), the Canadian Individual Poetry Slam (2016, 2017, 2019), and the Canadian Festival of Spoken Word, where they placed third nationally (2018). Kay currently resides on the unceded lands of the Musqueam, Squamish, and Tsleil-Waututh First Nations, colonially known as Vancouver, BC.

Contributors

LUX AETERNA is a retired stripper who worked a decade through New York and Florida, choosing to "fight with [her] clothes off," a hat-tip to *Stone Butch Blues*. A queer lesbian with PTSD due to a near-death experience, Lux chose this work after graduating from college *magna cum laude* and believes sex work is work. Lux currently spends her days working in advertising and her nights as a resin artist and activist. She has been performing her own poems with the New York City Poetry Brothel since 2014.

ANONYMOUS This piece was written during one of many rock bottoms, and I am grateful to be able to say it no longer echoes my sentiments toward sex or sex work. However, it provides an important, albeit gritty, perspective on the potential aftermath of sexual trauma that often goes unacknowledged: hypersexuality and sexual behaviors as self-harm.

JESSICA BARRY is a pseudonym under which the author writes fiction based on her experiences as an exotic dancer. She has a Ph.D. in cultural anthropology and currently works as a research consultant.

KRISTY LIN BILLUNI With roots in the sex industry, San Francisco writer and teacher Kristy Lin Billuni has aroused thousands of writers at her day job as The Sexy Grammarian. Prized credits include an essay forthcoming in *Sinister Wisdom*, fiction in *Leopardskin & Limes*, and her recent debut as a playwright on the Piano Fight cabaret stage.

CAM Using graphic design and short visual poetry, Cam expounds on the short-but-not-so-sweet dissociative sensation of interacting with trans fetishist clients and their queries.

CHRISTOPHER was born in Miami, and has used good luck and charm to make a living both at home and abroad. He is a musician and a music lover. He writes poetry.

DAVY LE JONES NGUYEN is a philosopher and poet currently living in Spokane, WA. They use their platform as a performer, organizer and educator to help bring awareness and interest to the possible ways in which each and every individual may become an agent of momentous change and significance. Their work features an intersection of trans-queer, biracial, and otherwise marginalized identities in poetry, seminars, and workshops. They will also write a poem about your dog.

ROBIN M. EAMES is a queercrip poet and historian living on Gadigal land (Sydney, Australia). You can find more of their work at robinmeames.org.

ROBIN GOW'S poetry has recently been published in POETRY, *Furrow*, *carte blanche*, FIVE:2:ONE, and *Corbel Stone Press*. He is a graduate student at Adelphi University pursing an MFA in creative writing. He runs two poetry blogs and interns for Porkbelly Press. He is an out and proud bisexual transgender man passionate about feminism and LGBTQ issues.

GIGI GENET'S poetry, fiction, and comics have been published in a variety of anthologies and literary journals across North America. She lives in Vancouver, BC and Los Angeles.

BEN JORISCH is just a speck on the face of the void.

MASON is a queer worker in western Canada who tries to keep growing but is reluctant to switch flowerpots. They push to make artwork accessible and to destigmatize even the messy side of mental illness, and they aren't about to stop anytime soon.

MATEO LARA is from Bakersfield, California. He received his B.A. in English at CSU Bakersfield, and is currently working on his M.F.A. in poetry at Randolph College in Lynchburg, VA. His poems have been featured in *Orpheus*, EOAGH, *Empty Mirror*, and

The New Engagement. He is an editor for the RabidOak online literary journal and Zoetic Press.

JULIA LAXER lives for the stories and writes in the afternoons from a messy desk in a rose-lit room in Portland, Oregon. She uses performance art and spiritual practice to explore archetype and ritual, and writes poems, essays, erotica, and memoir.

VIVIENNE L'CRAVE fancies herself a fat, femme, naked Robin Hood who uses her curves and words to profit from the patriarchy by commodifying her self-love through nude modeling and poetry. Cue trumpet fanfare.

VIVE L'OISEAU (they/them) is a French phrase that roughly means "long live the bird." The author exists under different names in different places, but is the kind of Aries who is always going to mention they're an Aries. Contact them at viveloiseau@gmail.com.

LIV MCKEE lives in upstate New York with chosen family and a boss baby. As a spoken word artist, dancer, musician, and maker, Liv revels in blurring lines between art forms. In 2018 she was commissioned to create and help implement Buffering, a poetry/dance fusion project about the end of the world. Liv tours, competes, and hosts workshops all over the northeastern so-called USA. She was a 2018 National Poetry Slam Team Piece Finalist with the first ever all-femme cohort of Albany's Nitty Gritty Slam, and has been a winning poet at numerous tri-state regional slams. She was a finalist in the 2017 Stephen A. DiBiase Poetry Contest, and has been featured on Write About Now!, Feminink, MZ TU POETRY, and in her two self-published chapbooks *honey at the corners of her mouths* and BULB. In her free time, Liv may be found having conversations with the moon and/or contemplating whorephobia. She hopes her poetry leaves you cut, bandaged, bathed, and heartened. Instagram: @livspoken

J. MORK is a longtime resident of San Francisco. She has written and performed in the Bay Area, focusing around issues of disability and sexuality. She has been a sex worker for 18 years, starting with a stint in phone sex at age 20. She has been published in *Dirty Old Women* and *Shivering in a Paper Gown: Breast Cancer and Its Aftermath*.

ZOEY MORRIS is an undergraduate student attending the University of Louisville, pursuing a degree in English. She is a queer woman and emerging writer, born and raised in Louisville, Kentucky, and is interested in exploring experimental poetry.

PEACE is a tenacious artist originally from Denver, Colorado, who now considers Houston home. Her writing style can be described as cutthroat wisdom, creating an experience that engages the audience and allows them to feel/heal freely based on interpretation. "There is a certain peace that one gets with speaking their mind and standing confidently behind their words and/or who they are. That is the type of peace I thrive to embody." —PeaceThePoet. Subjects of her voice include: motherhood, feminine empowerment, all BLACK everything, mental and emotional health, institutionalization, homeless eradication, heteronormative standards, womanism, business empowerment, and growth. Peace considers herself well-versed in a variety of important topics that may be hard to navigate.

J. RANDOM's hobbies include feeding the underbelly, getting paid for it, writing, and not getting paid for it.

RLYNN is a queer black poet in the Northeast. They love hip-hop and vegan mac and cheese, and they are heavily influenced by the voices of the Harlem Renaissance.

JUNE SAYERS A former lawyer but a lifetime artist, June has always used literature as her main means of expression. As a queer woman raised both conservative and Catholic, the discrimination and opposition she has faced led her to write primarily about marginalized and outcast women. This is her first publication, but one of her other short stories, "Billable Hours," was shortlisted for the 2018 Enter the Void Fiction Prize. You can check out her short stories and other creative projects at patreon.com/junesayers. She also posts about all her work on Twitter at @JuneSayers1.

CHRISTINA SPRINGER is an Alt.Black artist who uses text, performance, video, and other visual expressions to communicate what the spaces between molecules in the air wish for you to know. Cave Canem shaped her voice. Her book *The Splooge Factory* was released by Frayed Edge Press in November 2018. Christina's work "Futuristic Relics & Motherboards Sacred: a collection of 75 paintings, fabric and mixed media objects from a museum of our Black womanist utopian future," was recently shown in San Jose, Dayton and Pittsburgh. Her most recent theatrical offering, "She Diva Died. & Come Again?" incorporated text, movement, music, and video to explore the challenges and joys of raising a Black man. Her educational outreach work included four site-specific, mixed-media projects with youth at the Tower of London. Christina resides in Pittsburgh, PA, where she home educates her son.

STRAWBERRY is an escort and occasional massage "girl." They live in Victoria, BC, with their beautiful family and two cats. They like what they do, and it pays really freakin' well. Strawberry is a punk, a feminist, a student, a partner, a trans person, and YES, a sex worker. They're waiting for the day they can list their real job on a lease and the day they can stop crying while watching the news.

ANNA SUAREZ is a writer of poetry, fiction, and memoir. She explores themes of identity, embodiment, and interpersonal relationships through an erotic lens. She holds a bachelor's degree in philosophy and French from Portland State University. Her poetry collection, *Papi Doesn't Love Me No More*, published with CLASH Books, will be released in 2019.

Also by Thorntree Press

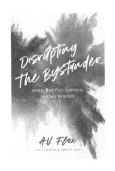

Disrupting the Bystander: When #metoo Happens Among Friends
A.V. Flox, with a foreword by Feminista Jones

"**Disrupting the Bystander** combines deep theory and intensely practical advice, creating an essential handbook for supporting those who have been harmed, while also caring for yourself. If you've ever felt helpless in the face of someone else's discomfort or pain, this book will teach you how to show up and stand up."
—Laszlo Bock, CEO of Humu and author of **Work Rules! Insights from Inside Google to Transform How You Live and Lead**

Ask: Building Consent Culture
Edited by Kitty Stryker, with a foreword by Laurie Penny and an afterword by Carol Queen

"There are certain conversations that deepen how you think; positively impact how you act; expand your view and understanding of the world, and forever alter how you approach it. This book is full of them. Make room for it—then spread the word."
—Alix Fox, journalist, sex educator and ambassador for the Brook sexual wellbeing charity

Love's Not Color Blind: Race and Representation in Polyamorous and Other Alternative Communities
Kevin A. Patterson

"It's incredibly hard to talk about racism with people who are not receptive to education. Kevin does amazing work in this book both centering the voices of people of color and educating white folks on privilege. His words will positively influence polyamorous communities for years to come."
—Rebecca Hiles, The Frisky Fairy and co-author of **It's Called "Polyamory": Coming Out About Your Nonmonogamous Relationships**

Love, Retold
Tikva Wolf

"Through both the drawings and the words, the reader will repeatedly be startled by how well Wolf captures the workings of the human heart and our attempts at deep connection and lasting love."
—Kathy Labriola, author of **The Polyamory Breakup Book**, **Love in Abundance**, and **The Jealousy Workbook**